Object Talks for Children
(ages 6 - 8)

by Sandra Crosser

STANDARD PUBLISHING
Cincinnati, Ohio

The Standard Publishing Company, Cincinnati, Ohio
A division of Standex International Corporation
© 1996 by Sandra Crosser
All rights reserved
Printed in the United States of America

04 03 02 01 99 98 97 96   5 4 3 2 1

All Scripture quotations, unless otherwise indicated, are taken from the HOLY BIBLE, NEW INTERNATIONAL VERSION® NIV®. Copyright © 1973, 1978, 1984 by International Bible Society. Used by permission of Zondervan Publishing House. All rights reserved.

Contents

Scripture	Theme	Page
Genesis 1:27	Nature of God	5
Genesis 1:31	God's Signature	6
Psalm 46:1	Trust in God	7
Psalm 113:2	God's Holy Name	8
Psalm 139:2, 4	Omniscient God	9
Proverbs 3:9	God's Plan for Money	10
Proverbs 12:22	Truthfulness	12
Isaiah 41:10	God Strengthens Us	13
Isaiah 41:10	Trusting in God's Presence	14
Isaiah 44:6	God's Name Is Holy	15
Micah 6:8	God's Leading	17
Micah 6:8	God's Requirements for Christian Life	19
Matthew 6:19-21	Materialism	20
Matthew 16:26	Christian Life	21
Matthew 22:37-39	Obedience	23
Mark 9:23	All Things Are Possible	24
John 6:47	Salvation	25
1 Corinthians 13:5	Love Is Not Selfish	27
Galatians 5:13	Free Will	28
Ephesians 3:17-19	Rooted in Faith	29
Ephesians 4:6	God in Us	30
Ephesians 4:31, 32	Serving God	32
Ephesians 6:1	Almighty God	33
Philippians 4:13	God's Strength	34
Hebrews 13:8	God Never Changes	36
James 2:17	The Gift of Time	37
James 4:8	God Keeps Promises	38
1 Peter 2:16	People as Tools of God	39
1 John 1:9	Forgiveness	40
1 John 1:9	Repentance	42
1 John 4:1-3	Jesus Is the Truth	43
1 John 4:7, 8	Showing Love	45
Revelation 1:3	Reading the Bible	46
Revelation 5:8	Prayers Please God	47

Nature of God

Scripture:
"So God created man in his own image, in the image of God he created him; male and female he created them" (Genesis 1:27).

Object: photograph
You will need to bring a Polaroid camera to class for this talk.

(Take a Polaroid photo of the group. While you are waiting for it to develop, tell the children that another word for a photograph is an image. Ask children if any of them have ever seen a photograph of God. Ask what they think God looks like.)

We can't be sure exactly what God looks like because no one has ever taken a photograph of God. But we can learn what God is like by looking at how we are made. *(Show the children the photograph you have taken of the group. Pass it around.)*

The Bible tells us that God made us in His own image. That means that God made us like himself in many ways. We are a kind of photograph of God. All of the good and wonderful things about us show us what God is like. We can see, so we know that God sees. We can hear and smell, so we know that God hears and smells. We can touch and taste and smile. We know that God can touch and taste and smile. We can laugh and cry. God can laugh and God can cry. We can think and care and serve. God thinks and cares and serves. God loves. We can love. We are made in the image of God.

God gave us bodies and hearts and minds and souls. We need to use our bodies and hearts and minds and souls in good ways—God's ways. Then when people look at us, they will see God's image in us. In everything we do, we must always try to show God's image.

Prayer:
God, help us be a picture of your image in all we do. Help us use our bodies and hearts and minds and souls to do good. Amen.

God's Signature

Scripture:
"God saw all that he had made, and it was very good" (Genesis 1:31). "The earth is the Lord's, and everything in it, the world, and all who live in it" (Psalm 24:1).

Object: painting or print
Choose a beautiful painting or print to use in this talk.

(Show the children the painting or print and tell what you think is beautiful about the picture.)

The artist who made this painting must have been proud of his/her work because she/he signed it right on the front. *(Point out the artist's signature and read the name aloud.)* Have you ever signed your name to something beautiful that you made? When we write our own name it is called our signature. Signature is another word for name.

When God made the earth, He liked what He made so He put His signature on it. The beautiful earth belongs to God so He signed His name to it in a very special way. Instead of using a pen or pencil to write His signature, God signed His name with beautiful flowers and trees and rivers and rocks. He signed His name to the earth by filling it with beautiful things. So every time you see a beautiful pebble or a snowflake or a flower, remember that God created the earth and all of the beautiful things in it. God made the earth and signed His name with beautiful things so we would know that He is God.

Prayer:
Dear God, we see what you have made all around us. We remember that you, alone, created a beautiful world. We see your signature in every beautiful sky and delicate flower. Your signature is on the earth. Amen.

Trust in God

Scripture:
"God is our refuge and strength, an ever-present help in trouble" (Psalm 46:1). "When I am afraid, I trust in you" (Psalm 56:3).

Object: bird figurine or picture
To make this talk especially appealing, bring a bird figurine to class. If one is not available, use a colorful bird picture.

(Hold up the figurine or picture and initiate a brief discussion about favorite birds.)

Did you ever see a bird perched on a branch or on a telephone wire? Some birds can even sleep while they are perched. Do you think you could sleep standing on a telephone wire? Why not? *(Accept responses.)*

Our bodies are not suited to standing on branches or wires, but birds' bodies are. When a bird lands on a perch, its feet wrap around the perch and its legs and feet lock in place. With its legs and feet locked, a bird won't fall off of the perch even if there is a storm and the wind is gusty. The bird can remain securely attached to the perch and go to sleep without fear of falling even during a storm.

God provides security for birds. He provides security for us, too. When trouble comes into our lives, we are like birds perched on a telephone wire during a storm. When we put our trust in God, we lock on tightly to Him just like the bird's legs and feet lock onto a perch. God is able to help us bear whatever trouble blows our way. He keeps us strong enough to withstand stormy times.

Everyone has trouble from time to time. That's just the way life is. But you will be able to move securely through your times of trouble when you trust God and lock on to Him.

Prayer:

Lord God, you alone are able to keep us strong in times of trouble. We trust you. We thank you for caring so much about each of us. Amen.

God's Holy Name

Scripture:

"Let the name of the Lord be praised, both now and forevermore" (Psalm 113:2).

Object: file folder and puppet

In large letters, print the words "Katherine Sue Buttermore" on one side of a file folder and on the other side of the folder print "God." Stand the file folder up with the words "Katherine Sue Buttermore" facing the children. *(Use a puppet to teach this lesson.)*

(The puppet enters and points to the file folder.)

Hi. This is my name. *(Pointing.)* My real name is Katherine but most of the time Mom and Dad call me Kathy. Sometimes they called me Sis, or Kitty, or even Honey, or Sweetie. All of those names are fine, but I especially like it when my parents called me Honey and Sweetie.

But if I forget to do my chores, or if I make a mess and don't clean it up, or if I leave my bike in the middle of the driveway, my parents use a different name. They use my full name: Katherine Sue Buttermore. And I know by the way they say it that I am not just being called to dinner. "Katherine Sue Buttermore," they say in a most stern and disagreeable tone. I don't like to hear that tone. It makes me nervous.

But the worst way they ever say my name is different still. The worst way they ever say my name is like this: "Oh, Katherine!" *(With disgust.)* I hate to hear my name spoken that way.

I think God must feel terrible sometimes when people say His name. *(Turn over the file folder to reveal the name, God.)* This is God's name. It is a holy and very special name, but I've heard people say, "Oh, God!" *(With disgust.)* in the same way my parents say, "Oh, Katherine." They say it like they have just tasted something rotten.

Have you ever heard God's name spoken that way? What do you think about that? *(Accept responses.)* God's name is holy. We need to speak His name with love and respect.

Prayer:
Heavenly Father, Holy God, you are worthy of honor. We love and respect your name. Amen.

Omniscient God

Scripture:
"You know when I sit and when I rise; you perceive my thoughts from afar. Before a word is on my tongue you know it completely, O Lord" (Psalm 139:2, 4).

Object: dictionary
Bring a large dictionary to class for this talk.

(Hold up the dictionary and ask what it is. Then ask what is in a dictionary. Accept responses.)

There are thousands of words in this dictionary. Usually we use some of these words when we pray. But sometimes when we are worried or sad, we don't know what words to use in our prayers. At times we don't know how to explain to God how we are feeling or what we need. Sometimes we just don't know the right words to tell God what is in our hearts.

But that is no problem for our mighty God! The Bible tells us that God knows each of us so well that He understands what is in our hearts even before we speak any words. God knows us that well. God loves us so much that He takes time to know all about us. God knows the way we feel. God knows what we need. God knows, even when we don't have the words to tell Him!

So, if you are ever so worried or so sad that you don't know what words to pray, just ask God to listen to your heart.

Prayer:
Dear God, thank you for knowing each of us and understanding how we feel. Thank you for knowing what is in our hearts even when we don't know the words to pray. Amen.

God's Plan for Money

Scripture:
"Honor the Lord with your wealth, with the firstfruits of all your crops" (Proverbs 3:9).

Object: money
Set out an offering plate, a child's bank, and a one dollar bill.

(Show children a one dollar bill and tell them you earned it and now you are trying to decide how you will use the dollar. Ask the children for suggestions.)

Thank you for the great ideas. God has a plan for my dollar, too. He wrote that plan in the Bible so everyone could know about it. I know that God's plans are always right for me. Let me tell you about God's plan for our money.

If I took my dollar to the bank and asked the banker to trade it for pennies, how many pennies should the banker give me? If I asked him to trade my dollar for all dimes, how many dimes should he give me? Let's pretend that I asked for dimes. *(Show the children a plastic bag with ten dimes in it.)*

Here are the ten dimes traded for my dollar. This is what God says I should do with these dimes. God's plan says that I should give away the very first dime to God. I'll put that one in the offering plate like the one we use in church service. How many dimes are left? Nine dimes are left. God's plan says I should save the next dime. I'll put that one in the bank. Now how many dimes are left? Eight dimes are left. God's plan says I can choose how to use those eight dimes. I gave one dime to God. I saved one, and now I have eight dimes left.

God's plan for our money is perfect. We may have a little money or we may have a lot of money. Even if we have only a little money, God's perfect plan is the same. The first part we use to serve God. The second part we save for later, and all the rest is left for us to save or spend as we choose. God's plans are always the best plans. So, if we're smart we'll follow God's plans for everything, even our money.

Prayer:

Dear God, thank you for your great money plan. Help us to give you the very first part, save the next part, and use the rest wisely. Amen.

Truthfulness

Scripture:
"The Lord detests lying lips, but he delights in men who are truthful" (Proverbs 12:22).

Object: two ropes
You will need two pieces of rope for this talk. One piece is just plain rope and the other has several knots tied in it.

(Show the children a piece of rope.)

This is a fine piece of rope. It is very useful to have a good piece of rope around. Rope can be used to tie a stack of newspapers together. It can be used to play jump rope or hold up a tire swing. A good piece of rope is also good for towing cars. Can you think of any other ways rope might be useful? *(Accept the children's responses, then show them another length of rope that has many knots tied in it.)*
I wonder how this rope got so many knots tied in it. The knots make it hard to use the rope. They get in the way and they make the rope shorter, too. These knots are hard to get out. A rope is not very useful when it is full of knots.
Our lives are like pieces of rope. Just like we can find lots of uses for a rope, God can find lots of uses for our lives. God wants to use our lives to draw people close to Him. God wants to use us in His work. But sometimes our lives get knotted up with lies. When our lives are full of lies, we are not very useful to God. Knots are hard to get out of a rope and lies are hard to get out of our lives. Knots are troublesome. Lies are troublesome. We need to be truthful so God can use us in His work. We need to remember that lies are like knots in a rope. They are nothing but trouble.

Prayer:
Dear God, sometimes it is hard to tell the truth. We know that you want us to be truthful. You don't want us to tell lies. Help us always to tell the truth. Amen.

God Strengthens Us

Scripture:
"So do not fear, for I am with you; do not be dismayed, for I am your God. I will strengthen you and help you; I will uphold you with my righteous right hand" (Isaiah 41:10).

Object: balloon
Before class place a deflated balloon on a table, leaving the mouthpiece hanging over the edge of the table. Secure a stack of three or four books with a rubber band and place the books on top of the balloon.

(Ask the children to look at your display of the deflated balloon and books carefully.)

This balloon has a heavy load on top of it. The books are so heavy that the balloon is pressed flat against the table. Is there a way to get the balloon out from under this heavy load without touching the books? Let's try blowing some air into the balloon. Watch what happens. *(As you blow into the balloon inflating it, the books will lift and fall away. It is a good idea to practice this before class.)*
Sometimes people are like this balloon, loaded down with heavy problems. Our problems can seem so heavy that we cannot get out from under them by ourselves. But when we have God in us, He gives us strength to get out from under the problems that weigh us down. The air strengthened the balloon and allowed it to get out from under the weight of the heavy books. God will strengthen us so we can get out from under our heavy problems. All

we have to do is ask God to strengthen us and He will.

Prayer:
> Dear God, we need your strength. Come into our lives and strengthen us. Help us to get out from under our problems. You are our strength. Amen.

Trusting in God's Presence

Scripture:
> "So do not fear, for I am with you; do not be dismayed, for I am your God. I will strengthen you and help you; I will uphold you with my righteous right hand" (Isaiah 41:10).

Object: riddles
> If you wish, write the riddles on individual cards before class to add interest and drama to your talk.

I hope you are feeling extra smart this morning because today is riddle day. Dust off your brain and get ready for the first riddle. Here it comes.

> What food can shout? (ice cream)
> Here is another riddle. Try this one.
> What has a trunk but doesn't have a car? (elephant)
> Here is the hardest one of all. Are you ready?
> What is all around but never seen? (air)

(Compliment the children on their skill at solving riddles.)

That last riddle got me to thinking. Air is a lot like God. We cannot see air and we cannot see God, but they are both all around us wherever we go. We know that air exists because we can see it working. When we put air into a flat tire, we can see the tire get bigger. When we blow air into a balloon, we see the balloon expand. When we blow air through a straw, we see it make bubbles in our drinks. When air moves fast, we can feel it in our hair and on our skin. And when air moves really fast, it can even break branches off of trees.

We can move air with a fan. We can even smash air. *(Clap your hands together loudly.)* When I clapped my hands, I smashed the air and it made a sound. You try it.

We know that air is all around us even though we cannot see it. God is all around us, too, even though we cannot see Him. We can see God at work just like we can see the air at work. We can see the beautiful world that God made. God promised to send Jesus and we can see that He did. We can see God's work as He answers our prayers and gives us courage. We can feel God close to us when we read the Bible and worship Him.

Yes, God is real. He is always with us. We can see the work He does.

Prayer:
Our Heavenly Father, help us to remember that you are here and you are working all around us. We are thankful for all that you do for us. Amen.

God's Name Is Holy

Scripture:
"This is what the Lord says—Israel's King and Redeemer, the Lord Almighty: I am the first and I am the last; apart from me there is no God" (Isaiah 44:6).

Object: names
Before children arrive, print the following name on a poster or chart paper: Adolph Blaine Charles David Earl Frederick Gerald Hubert Irvin John Kenneth Lloyd Martin Nero Oliver Paul Quincy Randolph Sherman Thomas Uncas Victor William Xerxes Yancy Zeus Wolfeschlegelsteinhausenbergerdorffvoralternwarenge

wissenhaftschaferswessenschafewarenwohlgepflegeundsorgfaltigkeitbeschutzenvonangreifendurcheinenvanderersteerdemenschderraumschiffgebrauchlichtalsseinursprungvonkraftgestartseinlangefahrthinzwischensternartigraumaufdersuchenachdiesternwelchegehabtbewohnbarplanetenkreisedrehensichundwohinderneurassevonverstandigmenschlichkeitkonntefortflanzenundsicherfreuenanlebenslanglichfreudeundruhemitnichteinfurchtvorangreifenvonandererintelligentgeschopfsvonhinzwischensternartigraum.

(Ask the children how many names they have. Accept all responses. Have children tell their full names if they know them. Ask children if they have any nicknames.)

(Hold up the chart you have made so the back is facing the children. Tell them that you have written the longest name in the world on the chart. Have children guess how long the name is. Turn over the chart and try to read the name together.)

(Tell the children that, according to the Guinness Book of World Records, the man who owns this name lives in Pennsylvania. He has 26 first names and it takes 590 letters to spell his last name. He got so tired of writing his last name that he decided to just write it Wolfe+585.)

Did you know that Jesus has more than one name? God has more than one name, too. Let's see how many of their names you know.

(On a large piece of chart paper or on a chalkboard write "God" on the top left and "Jesus" on the top right. As children tell the other names they know for God and Jesus, record them in the appropriate column. When children can think of no more names, give each child a "Post-It" note and a pencil.)

We need some grown-ups to help us finish the chart. If you grown-ups know another name for God or Jesus, raise your hand high in the air.

(Send children out to collect those names on their "Post-It" notes and add the new names to the chart. When you have collected all of the names from the grown-ups, lead the children in reading the chart. Challenge the children to collect more names during the week to add to the chart next time they meet.)

All of these names are holy. The Bible tells us in Psalm 99:3 that God's name is holy. *(Read Psalm 99:3.)* Whenever we hear these names, we know they all are ways of saying God's holy name or Jesus' holy name.

Your list might include the following names for God: Jehovah, Lord, I Am, Yahweh, Father, Holy One of Israel, Most High, Mighty One, He, Heavenly Father, Almighty, Mighty King, Alpha and Omega, Shepherd of Israel.

Names for Jesus: Lord, Emanuel, Rabbi, Prince of Peace, Savior, Son of God, Messiah, King of Kings, Lord of Lords, Redeemer, Master, Root of Jesse, Good Shepherd, Teacher, Lamb of God, Lion of Judah, Christ, Root of David, Jesus of Nazareth.

Prayer:
> Dear God, we know your name is holy. We know Jesus' name is holy. You are mighty. You are the one and only God. Amen.

God's Leading

Scripture:
> "He has showed you, O man, what is good. And what does the Lord require of you? To act justly and to love mercy and to walk humbly with your God" (Micah 6:8).

Object: toy dog
> Find an old, dirty stuffed toy dog. Put a Band-Aid on the dog and rub bits of leaves and grass into its fur.

(Hold up the toy dog and introduce him as Max.)

Yesterday Max wanted to go for a walk in the woods. His master clipped a leash onto Max's collar and set off for what should have been a nice walk down the grassy trails through the woods. Max's master knew the way to go and he knew that it was important to stay on the trails. The trails are good to walk on, but getting off of the trails only means trouble. Off of the trails there are sticker bushes, burrs, and wet, muddy spots. There is poison ivy off the trails and it is easy to trip over stumps and fallen branches that are hidden in the weeds.

Max was excited about putting on his leash because he knew it meant he was going for a walk. His master led the way and Max walked close behind. Everything was going just fine until a big, brown rabbit hopped across the trail in front of them. That was the end of the quiet walk.

What do you think Max did? Yes, Max took off after that rabbit, pulling the leash right out of his master's hand. "Max!" his master called, "Max, come back!"

But Max didn't listen. He was too busy chasing that rabbit through the woods, through the sticker bushes, through the burrs, through the mud, and through the poison ivy. Max ran fast and he was gaining on the rabbit until Max tripped over a fallen branch and tumbled headlong into the weeds. "Yip, yip, yip," Max cried.

Carefully Max got up and limped back to where his master was standing on the trail. What a sight he was! Max had burrs and weeds in his fur; he had a thorn in his foot; and he was covered all over with mud. Max had gone off on his own and all he had found was trouble.

Our lives are a lot like a walk in the woods. God has cleared the good trails and wants to be our master and lead us His way. But sometimes people choose to leave God's way and run off on their own way just like Max. Max tried to lead the way and only found trouble. Max needs to follow his master. We need to follow our master, too. We need to follow God or we will find ourselves in trouble, just like Max. God knows the way. We need to follow Him.

Prayer:
> Father in Heaven, help us live our lives following you. Keep us from running off on our own ways. Lead us and help us be good followers. Amen.

God's Requirements for Christian Life

Scripture:
> "He has showed you, O man, what is good. And what does the Lord require of you? To act justly and to love mercy and to walk humbly with your God" (Micah 6:8).

Object: scout uniforms
> Collect a variety of scout uniforms from the organizations popular with children in your area. You may want to borrow only shirts, or caps, or scarves from Cub Scouts, Bluebirds, Brownies, etc.

(Hold up the parts of the uniforms of scouting organizations you have borrowed. Ask the children if any of them are in scouting or if they know anyone who is a scout.)

Are there any requirements to be a scout? Are there any things scouts must do? *(Accept responses, then summarize what the children have said including requirements such as: (1) attend meetings; (2) share the work; (3) do projects; (4) earn badges; (5) pay dues.)*

If someone wants to be a scout, there are certain things he/she must do. Those things are called requirements. *(Hold up a scout handbook.)*

This book tells all of the requirements to be a scout. Boy Scouts, Cub Scouts, Brownies, and Campfire Girls and Boys all have handbooks to tell them the requirements.

God has requirements, too. God's people need to do

what God requires. *(Hold up a Bible.)* This is God's handbook for His people. The Bible tells us God's requirements. When we read the Bible, we find out God's requirements so we can do them. In the Bible God has told us what is good. God requires us to be fair and kind and to follow wherever He leads us. We need to study God's handbook so we know His requirements. Then we must do what God requires.

Prayer:
Dear God, we want to be fair and kind. Help us follow your requirements and live our lives so they are pleasing to you. Amen.

Materialism

Scripture:
"Do not store up for yourselves treasures on earth, where moth and rust destroy, and where thieves break in and steal. But store up for yourselves treasures in heaven, where moth and rust do not destroy, and where thieves do not break in and steal. For where your treasure is, there your heart will be also" (Matthew 6:19-21).

Object: rusty toy
You will need an old toy, such as a truck, that has rust on it.
Adapt the talk to fit the toy being used.

(Show the children the rusty truck or other toy.)

When this toy was new, it looked great. The paint was shiny and smooth. It was a very nice looking truck. But look at what has happened. Look at all of this brown stuff that has ruined the truck. Do you know what it is? *(Accept responses.)* Yes, trucks and bicycles and even cars rust over time.

It is fun to have things like this toy truck, but we know that things won't last forever. Some things get rusty, others get torn, and others get broken. Things don't last. Jesus tells us not to be concerned with getting things because they will soon be gone or ruined. Instead, we should be concerned with doing good deeds for others. When we do good deeds, we build treasures that will last forever.

In the Bible Jesus tells us, "Do not store up for yourselves treasures on earth, where moth and rust destroy, and where thieves break in and steal. But store up for yourselves treasures in heaven, where moth and rust do not destroy, and where thieves do not break in and steal. For where your treasure is, there your heart will be also" (Matthew 6:19-21).

When all we think about is having things, our hearts become stuck on earth. But when we show our love for others, our hearts are heavenly.

Prayer:
> Lord, let us be people who build lasting treasures in Heaven. Help us remember to build treasures in Heaven by doing good for others. Amen.

Christian Life

Scripture:
> "What good will it be for a man if he gains the whole world, yet forfeits his soul?" (Matthew 16:26).

Object: water
> You will need to prepare for this lesson by freezing water in three containers of different shapes. In addition, you will need a glass of water, an oblong glass baking dish, and a square glass baking dish.

(Arrange the frozen water and other items in the order they will be used in your talk.)

I have a difficult question for you today, but you are a smart group. I think you will know the answer. Get your brains in gear. Are you ready? Here's the question: What shape is water? *(Accept responses.)*

(Hold up a clear glass of water.) What shape is this water? *(Pour the water into an oblong baking dish.)* Now what shape is the water? *(Pour the water into a square baking dish.)* Now what shape is the water?

I froze water in some containers. *(Show the children the containers and individually remove the ice from each, exploring the shapes of the ice and the relationships of the ice to their containers. Establish with the children the fact that water takes the shape of its container.)*

Water takes the shape of whatever container it is in. Our lives do the same thing. Our lives take the shape of whatever we put them in. If we put our lives in the world's container, we become like the world. We become concerned with selfish things like getting more toys, having more money, wearing fancy clothes, being good looking, being good at sports, and impressing people. All of those things are the world's container. That's not good because none of those things will last.

We need to put our lives in God's container so our lives will take the shape God wants them to. When we are in God's container, we become more like God. We become concerned with others, not just ourselves. We become concerned with helping, sharing, fairness, and loving. That's good because all of those things will last forever. Let's ask God to shape our lives in His container.

Prayer:

Dear God, it is easy to fall into the world's container, wanting more and more things for ourselves. Help us to love what you love, not what the world loves. Shape our lives to be more like you. Amen.

Obedience

Scripture:
"Jesus replied, 'Love the Lord your God with all your heart and with all your soul and with all your mind. This is the first and greatest commandment. And the second is like it: Love your neighbor as yourself'" (Matthew 22:37-39).

Object: toy soldier
You will need a toy soldier for this talk. One can probably be borrowed from a child's collection.

(Hold up toy soldier.)

This soldier just joined the army. He wants very much to be a good soldier—the best he can be. What kinds of things will he need to do if he is to be a good soldier? *(Accept responses.)*

(Summarize the responses of the children.) There are many things our soldier must do, but the most important thing he must do is always obey orders. When the commander gives orders to march, all of the soldiers must march. When the commander gives orders to halt, all of the soldiers must stop. When the commander gives orders to pitch a tent or wash a jeep, that's what good soldiers do.

Can good soldiers choose whether or not they will do as they are commanded? No! Soldiers must always follow commands. They can't say, "I'm too tired to march" or "I'm too busy to pitch a tent" or "I don't feel like washing the jeep." A command is not a choice. A command means do it now. Soldiers do what they are commanded.

Christians are God's soldiers. You and I are God's soldiers and God is the commander. We are not allowed to choose which of God's commandments to obey. We must obey all of God's commandments, just like other soldiers must always obey. Jesus said that God has two great commandments. Because God commands, we must obey. God commands us to love Him and God commands us to love other people. We can't choose to love some people and not others. God has commanded us to love. We must love people who are nice to us, but God also commanded us to love people who are not nice to us. God doesn't allow us to choose when to love or who to love. We are God's soldiers and He commands us to love.

It can be a tough job being God's soldiers. But we don't need to do it alone. Good commanders stand by their soldiers. God will stand by us. He will help us to be good Christian soldiers and follow His orders to love.

Prayer:

Lord God, help us obey your commandments. We love you. Help us to love others. Amen.

All Things Are Possible

Scripture:

"If you can?" said Jesus. "Everything is possible for him who believes" (Mark 9:23).

Object: Möbius loop

Cut sheets of plain paper lengthwise into one inch strips. You will need pencils for the children too.

(Give each child a strip of paper and a pencil. Then have each child write his/her name in the center of the paper and on the other side, write God's name. When finished, the child's name will be opposite God's name.)

(Instruct the children to hold both ends of the paper strip in their fingers. Demonstrate. Give one end of the paper half a twist. Overlap the ends, then tape the ends together. Help as needed. Tell the children that they have just made a Möbius loop.)

You wrote two names on the paper. On one side you wrote your name and on the other side you wrote God's name. The names were on opposite sides of the strip of paper. Let's see if they are still on opposite sides of the paper. Put one thumb on your name. Now slide your thumb along the paper until it comes to more writing. When you get to more writing, lift your thumb and see what the writing says. Don't lift your thumb off of the paper until you come to more writing. *(After completing the experiment, ask children to tell what happened. They should see that, without lifting their thumbs from the paper, they moved from their own name to God's name even though both names were originally on opposite sides of the paper.)*

Sometimes things that seem impossible really do happen. When we seem far away from God and our problems seem impossible to solve, God can get to us wherever we are. Keep your Möbius loop to remind you that all things are possible with God. God can move through the world to wherever you are, even if it seems impossible.

Prayer:
Lord God, we know that all things are possible for you. You are mighty and you are wise. Amen.

Salvation

Scripture:
"I tell you the truth, he who believes has everlasting life" (John 6:47).

Object: invitation
Prepare a paper invitation for yourself and one for each of the children. Inside each invitation print, "You are invited to Heaven. RSVP." Place the invitations in envelopes on which you have printed the children's names.

(Hold up the envelope containing your invitation. Be enthusiastic as you describe it.)

Did you ever get one of these in the mail? It is fun to get mail! I wonder what is inside the envelope. My name is written on it, so it is OK for me to open it. *(Open the envelope.)*
This looks like an invitation. Did you ever get an invitation in the mail? What kind of invitations have you received? Did you ever give anyone an invitation? Why? *(Accept responses.)*
This invitation is very special. It's not an invitation to a birthday party; it's not an invitation to a wedding; it's not an invitation to a baby shower; and it's not an invitation to an anniversary party. Listen to what it says. *(Read the invitation out loud.)*
When our time is finished on earth, God wants us to come to Heaven and be with Him forever. He sent Jesus into the world a long time ago so that you and I and all of the people of the world could be invited to Heaven when our lives are finished. Jesus died on the cross for us so we can go to Heaven and be with God forever.
This invitation says, "You are invited to Heaven." But it says more. It says "RSVP." Sometimes invitations say RSVP. What do those letters mean? *(Accept responses.)* When the letters RSVP are on an invitation, it means we need to tell the person if we accept the invitation. RSVP means tell me if you will come.
God invited us to Heaven when He sent Jesus to die for our sins, but we have to RSVP first. We need to tell God that we accept His invitation. When we believe in Jesus, we RSVP to God's invitation. When we believe in Jesus, we accept God's invitation. Here is your invitation to Heaven. *(Hand out invitations to all of the children.)*
Let's pray and RSVP to accept God's invitation.

Prayer:
Dear God, we accept your invitation to Heaven. We believe in Jesus. Thank you for sending Jesus. Amen.

Love Is Not Selfish

Scripture:
"Love is not self-seeking" (1 Corinthians 13:5).

Object: strips of paper
Cut two strips of paper about 8 inches long for this demonstration.

(Hold up the two strips of paper.)

What do you think will happen if I blow between these papers? *(Accept responses.)*

(Hold the paper strips on edge in front of your face and space them 4 or 5 inches apart. Blow steadily between the papers. The strips of paper will move inward, toward each other.)

What happened to the papers? Did you see how the papers moved inward, toward each other?
Tom and Jim are like these two strips of paper. They never agree because they each want their own way. Tom wants to go to a movie but Jim wants to go bowling. Tom wants to go to Pizza Hut but Jim wants a Burger King. Neither boy will give in, so they get separated by anger just like these two strips of paper are separated. But if Tom and Jim were to show God's love, they would not insist on their own way. The Bible tells us, "Love is not self-seeking." It does not insist on its own way. We show God's love when we let other people have their way.
When God's love blows between people, they are drawn closer to each other just like these two pieces of paper. *(Blow between the two strips of paper once again to demonstrate the inward movement.)*
Sometimes we are selfish and insist on our own way. When that happens we need to remember to show God's love by blowing away that selfishness, because love does not insist on its own way.

Prayer:
> Lord, help us show your love. Keep us from being selfish by insisting on our own way. Amen.

Free Will

Scripture:
> "You, my brothers, were called to be free. But do not use your freedom to indulge the sinful nature; rather, serve one another in love" (Galatians 5:13).

Object: marionette
> You will need a marionette for this talk. If one is not available, you can use a doll with strings tied to its limbs.

(Demonstrate how the marionette works. Invite two or three children to manipulate the marionette.)

The person who made this doll planned for it to be a marionette. She carefully tied strings to each arm and leg so she could make the marionette do whatever she wanted. She could make it walk or dance or wave or stand still just by pulling on the strings. The lady who made the marionette planned to simply stand above it and decide how it would move.

When God made you, He could have tied invisible strings to your arms and legs. He could have tied invisible strings to your mouth. But He didn't. God could have made us so we could only do or say what He wants us to do or say. God could have made us so we could only do good things. God could have made us like marionettes.

But God is very wise. He doesn't want us to be marionettes. God wants us to be free to choose what we do and what we say. He wants us to do good things and say good words. God made us so we can choose what to do and what to say. God loves us so much that He gives us choices.

He hopes we will show we love Him by choosing good ways to talk and good ways to move.

But sometimes people make bad choices. Sometimes people choose to hurt. And sometimes they hurt us. God doesn't want us to be hurt. God lets people choose to be hurters or helpers. Helpers please God. When people choose to hurt, it makes God sad.

Prayer:
God, help all of us choose to be helpful and good. Thank you for giving us choices. Amen.

Rooted in Faith

Scripture:
"So that Christ may dwell in your hearts through faith. And I pray that you, being rooted and established in love, may have power together with all the saints, to grasp how wide and long and high and deep is the love of Christ and to know this love that surpasses knowledge—that you may be filled to the measure of all the fullness of God" (Ephesians 3:17-19).

Object: roots
You will need to find a plant to uproot. Weeds with strong root systems make fine examples.

(Show the children the roots of the plant that you have brought to class.)

This plant has a strong root system. *(Point out the roots.)* What do the roots do for a plant? *(Accept responses.)*

Roots hold the plant firmly in the ground. They also carry nutrition and water from the soil to all of the other parts of the plant. If a plant doesn't have roots, it will not grow to be strong and healthy. People, too, need roots. You and I need roots. Plants need roots in the ground, but we don't need to be rooted in the ground. We need to be rooted in our faith if we are to grow and be healthy as Christians. How do we get rooted in our faith? *(Accept responses.)*

We become more strongly rooted in our faith when we learn about God. We learn about God when we read the Bible and come to Sunday school and church where we listen and ask questions. We need to do all we can to learn about how to be the best Christians we can be. Then we will grow stronger and stronger roots in our faith.

Prayer:
Lord, teach us your ways that we might grow strong roots. Amen.

God in Us

Scripture:
"One God and Father of all, who is over all and through all and in all" (Ephesians 4:6). "I in them and you in me. May they be brought to complete unity to let the world know that you sent me and have loved them even as you have loved me" (John 17:23).

Object: salad dressing
Bring a clear bottle with a lid, a measuring cup, vinegar, and cooking oil.

(Set out the supplies you have assembled for this talk. If you like, wear an apron or a chef's hat.)

Hello, boys and girls. I am the famous Chef Tasty Tater. Welcome to my kitchen. You are just in time to help me make my gourmet salad dressing. I'm so glad you came. This is a very famous recipe kept secret by the greatest cooks in the world. I will share this recipe with you because you are my friends. Are you ready to begin? First we need to measure one cup of salad oil. *(Help a child measure one cup of salad oil and pour it into the empty bottle.)*

Next, we need a half cup of vinegar. *(Help a child measure a half cup of vinegar and add it to the oil already in the bottle.)* Now put on the lid. Next comes the secret part. Can you keep a secret? *(Whisper.)* The secret is in shaking. Yes, shaking. You must shake the bottle seven times. *(Hold up the bottle.)* See how the oil and vinegar have separated? Oil and vinegar don't mix unless we shake the bottle. *(Select a child to shake the bottle seven times, then have the children observe the mixture.)*

What did the oil and vinegar look like before we shook the bottle? What does the oil and vinegar look like now after we have shaken the bottle? Look closely now and see if the oil and vinegar stay mixed together. What is happening?

Oil and vinegar separate. If we want them to mix, we have to shake them together, but they only stay mixed for a short time. Oil and vinegar dressing makes salad taste good, but we need to remember to shake it before we use it.

Some people want to be like oil and vinegar in their relationship with God. Some people want God to stay separate from them like the oil and vinegar stay separate. Some people want to be like the vinegar and just let God float around separate from them like the oil. Some people just don't understand that God can come into our lives and be in us, all mixed together with us, all of the time. When God comes into our lives, He will never separate from us like the oil and vinegar separated. God stays mixed into us and becomes part of us forever. We can trust God to always be part of us.

Prayer:

Lord God, come into our lives and be in us. Be part of us forever. Amen.

Serving God

Scripture:
"Get rid of all bitterness, rage and anger, brawling and slander, along with every form of malice. Be kind and compassionate to one another, forgiving each other, just as in Christ God forgave you" (Ephesians 4:31, 32).

Object: pebbles and pan or tub of water
Collect a few pebbles and a wide tub or pan of water before class begins.

(Have a child drop one of the pebbles into the water as the children watch what happens to the surface of the water. Repeat the activity until all of the children have had an opportunity to observe the ripples.)

What shape does each ripple make? *(Circle.)* What direction does the ripple move? *(Away from the spot where the pebble drops into the water.)* What would happen to the ripples if we were to drop two pebbles into the water at the same time? *(Drop two pebbles into the water at the same time and observe the ripples as they move through each other.)*

Our lives have a ripple effect, too. The way we live our lives affects other people just like ripples in water affect each other. When we are mean, our meanness ripples away from us and affects the people around us. When we are kind, our kindness ripples away from us and into the lives of the people around us. We can choose to be loving and kind, or we can choose to be mean and selfish. Whatever way we choose to live will affect the lives of the people around us. We serve God when we are kind, tenderhearted, and forgiving. When we serve God, His goodness ripples away from our lives and into the lives of everyone around us.

The Bible puts it this way "Get rid of all bitterness, rage and anger, brawling and slander, along with every form of malice. Be kind and compassionate to one another, forgiving each other, just as in Christ God forgave you" (Ephesians 4:31, 32).

Prayer:
Lord, help us serve you. Let us be kind, tenderhearted, and forgiving. Let your love show in everything we do so we can send ripples of your love and goodness into other people's lives. Amen.

Almighty God

Scripture:
"Children, obey your parents in the Lord, for this is right" (Ephesians 6:1). "But I gave them this command: Obey me, and I will be your God and you will be my people. Walk in all the ways I command you, that it may go well with you" (Jeremiah 7:23).

Object: chunk of ice
Freeze a chunk of ice and chip it into an irregular shape. Place it in a clear bowl. Add enough water to allow the ice to float freely.

(Draw the children's attention to the ice in the bowl.)

Look closely at this chunk of ice floating in the water. Is more of the ice sticking up out of the water? Is more of the ice under the water? *(Accept responses.)* Yes, we can see that most of the ice is under the water. Icebergs like this float in cold parts of the ocean. Sometimes ships crash into icebergs. Crashing into an iceberg would mean big trouble for a ship.

If there were a ship in our bowl of water, would the ship's captain be able to see all of the ice? What part would he be able to see? What would the captain need to do to be sure his ship would not crash into the hidden part of the iceberg? *(Accept responses.)*

Icebergs are trouble for ships so captains steer far away from them. Smart captains try to never come close to icebergs because they know that there is a lot of dangerous ice hidden under the water.

As we go through life we are a lot like ships sailing on the ocean. We need to steer far away from trouble just like a ship's captain needs to steer far away from icebergs. We cannot always see how much trouble there really is because part of it is hidden just like much of the iceberg is hidden.

God is a smart captain. He knows where all of the icebergs are. God tells us to obey Him and to obey our parents. When we obey God and our parents, we steer far away from trouble. God said that telling a lie is a trouble iceberg. Can you think of any other trouble icebergs? *(Accept responses.)*

Prayer:
Dear God, help us to obey you and help us to obey our parents so we can steer clear of troubles. Thank you. Amen.

God's Strength

Scripture:
"I can do everything through him who gives me strength" (Philippians 4:13).

Object: lever
Before the children arrive, tie a rope securely around a stack of heavy books or blocks to act as a weight. Have available a sturdy chair with a straight back and a handle from a mop or broom.

I am feeling especially strong today. In fact, I feel so strong that I think I can lift this heavy weight with just one finger. *(Invite two or three children to try.)*

(After the children have exhausted their ideas for lifting the weight with one finger, bring out the chair and mop or broom handle. Center the handle over the back of the chair. Put the end of the handle under the knot of the rope you have used to tie the bundle together. By pushing down with one finger on the opposite end of the handle you should be able to lift the weight with ease. Hint: The closer the chair is to the weight, the easier it will be to lift the weight.)

(Explain to the children that you have used a machine called a lever to help you lift the weight. Invite a few children to try using the lever to lift the weight with one finger. Experiment with placement of the chair to demonstrate that the chair, or support, works better as it is moved closer to the weight.)

God wants to be a lever in our lives. Sometimes we have problems that are too heavy or difficult for us to solve alone. God can make our problems easier to solve. When we pray to God and ask Him to help us solve our problems, He is like the chair in our lever experiment. Our prayers place God right between us and the problem. The closer God is to the problem, the easier it is for us to handle. Our prayers are invitations for God to help us.

Prayer:

Dear God, we know that you are very strong—strong enough to solve our problems and move all of the heavy weights in our lives. We pray that you will get between us and our problems. Help us remember to invite you to help us when we are not strong enough to do it alone. Thank you for wanting to help us. Amen.

God Never Changes

Scripture:
"Jesus Christ is the same yesterday and today and forever" (Hebrews 13:8).

Object: photographs
For this talk you will need to collect photographs of yourself when you were an infant, a toddler, a school-age child, and a teenager.

(Show the children the photographs of yourself in the various stages of your life. Briefly tell them what you liked to do at each age and what you wanted to be when you grew up. Then tell the children what you like to do now and what type of work you do.)

People change and grow. You are changing and growing. I have changed in what I look like, what I like to do, and even changed my mind about what I wanted to be when I grew up. You are changing and growing, too. You will change how you look and what you think as you grow. People change.

We can't be sure what we will be like as we constantly grow and change. But there is One who will never change. There is One who will always be the same. The Bible tells us that God is always the same. He will never change. God will always love us. God will always forgive us. God will always be holy and good, just like He is today. God will be the same tomorrow and a year from now. God will be the same in a thousand years. God will be the same forever. We can always depend on God to be the same. He will never change. We can count on God's love, mercy, and goodness.

Prayer:
Lord God, we are thankful that we can depend on you to always be the same loving, good, and merciful God that you are today. Amen.

The Gift of Time

Scripture:
"In the same way, faith by itself, if it is not accompanied by action, is dead" (James 2:17).

Object: a five dollar bill and an hourglass
You will need a five dollar bill or another denomination for this talk. Adapt to fit the type of money you use.

(Hold up a five dollar bill. Ask the children to tell what they would do with a five dollar bill if someone gave it to them. Accept all responses. If no one has mentioned saving the money, ask how many people might save all or part of the money.)

If someone were to give me a gift of a five dollar bill, I would think that was great! There are lots of choices for ways to use it. But did you know that God gave each of us a gift worth even more than a five dollar bill—a gift worth even more than a hundred dollar bill? He gave us each a gift of time. God gave us each a gift of a lifetime of minutes and hours and days and years. And God lets us choose how to spend every moment of our lifetimes. We can spend our time wisely or we can waste it. There is only one thing we cannot do with our time. The only thing we cannot do with our time is to save it.

(Show the children an hourglass. Tiny hourglasses are available in household gadget sections of discount stores. Ask the children to describe how an hourglass works.)

Once we turn the hourglass over, the sand keeps falling into the bottom. There is no way to save up the sand in the top part. The sand just keeps on moving. We can't save time in our lives either. Time keeps on moving, and we can never get minutes or hours or days or years back again after we spend them.

Yes, time is a very valuable gift from God. He hopes we will spend our time wisely and not waste it. It pleases God when we spend our time wisely. You are spending your time wisely this morning by choosing to be in church learning about God and worshiping Him. What other ways can you spend your time wisely?

Prayer:
Thank you, God, for your gift of time. Help us value our time and spend it wisely. Help us spend our time to do good, to help others, and to worship and learn about you. Amen.

God Keeps Promises

Scripture:
"Come near to God and he will come near to you" (James 4:8).

Object: magnet
You will need to use a paper clip with the magnet in this talk to show God's promise to us.

(Place a magnet on a smooth, flat surface where the children can see it.)

Do you know what happens when a paper clip gets close to a magnet? Let's watch and see. I'll use this pencil eraser to move the paper clip slowly toward the magnet. When the paper clip gets close enough, the magnet will pull the paper clip to itself.

As the paper clip came close to the magnet, the magnetic force pulled the paper clip up to the magnet. Our relationship with God is like this paper clip and magnet. When we move close to God, He pulls us even closer to Him. We are like the paper clip and God is like the magnet. God wants us to be close to Him. The Bible says, "Come near to

God and he will come near to you" (James 4:8). That means God promises that if we come close to Him, He will come close to us. And God always keeps His promises.

How can you move close to God? You move near to God every time you pray and every time you are quiet and think about Him. You can move near to God when you sing to Him or read the Bible. Those are times He will come close to you. What a loving, wonderful God we have.

(Give each child a paper clip as a reminder of God's promise.)

Prayer:
Our God, we want to move close to you now. We trust that you will come near to us because you always keep your promises. Amen.

People as Tools of God

Scripture:
"Live as servants of God" (1 Peter 2:16).

Object: tools
Prepare for this talk by placing a few common hand tools such as a hammer, screwdriver, carpenter's rule, drill, plane, or file into a small toolbox.

(Show the children the toolbox.)

Who might need a box like this to do their work? Why? *(Accept responses.)* Someone who needs to build or repair things might need a box like this. *(Open the toolbox and take out the tools individually, asking what each tool is called and how it is used.)*

Each of these tools is useful in its own way. Each has its own special purpose, but all of these tools do important work.

God uses tools, too. But God does not use hammers and

screwdrivers to do His work. Instead, God chooses you and me and all Christians everywhere to be His tools. God knows each of us can do a special kind of work for Him. God uses people as tools to help others. We are useful tools for God when we show love and kindness. And we are God's tools when we help others learn about Jesus. Remember, whenever you do good for others and share Jesus' love you are being a tool of God. God can use you to do His very important work.

Prayer:
Dear Father in Heaven, use us as tools to do your work. Use us to show your loving kindness. Amen.

Forgiveness

Scripture:
"If we confess our sins, he is faithful and just and will forgive us our sins and purify us from all unrighteousness" (1 John 1:9).

Object: filters
Collect two glass jars, four coffee filter papers, a small pitcher of water, and five or six dirty pebbles.

(Be sure all the children can easily see the experiment being performed.)

Today we are going to do an experiment to help us learn about God's forgiveness. You may help. First, we need to pour some water into one of these jars so it will be about half full. *(Call on a child to pour the water.)* This is clean, clear water. It is clean enough to drink. God wants our souls to be this clean. Now we are going to add some pebbles to the water. These are ordinary pebbles like you could find in your yard or in a parking lot. *(Call on a child to add the peb-*

bles to the water in the jar, then have someone cap the jar and secure the lid.)

What does our mixture look like now? *(Accept responses.)*

We are a lot like this jar of water. When we sin or do things that are wrong, it is like putting dirty pebbles into our lives. Each time we are selfish, unkind, or tell a lie, or hurt someone, we are putting another dirty sin into our souls just like we put dirty pebbles into the clean water. And, sadly, we all do sin. *(Shake the jar containing the pebbles.)*

Sin makes us dirty before God. We need to get rid of the sin in our lives so we can be clean before God. But we can't do it by ourselves. We need Jesus. When Jesus died on the cross, He made it possible for us to get rid of all of our sins so we can be clean before God. If we ask Jesus to forgive us for our sins, He will take away each of the sins that make our souls dirty like this dirty water. He will make us clean. It works something like this. *(Insert four coffee filter papers into the top of the empty jar and pour the dirty water and pebbles into the filter, holding the filter in place.)*

But look at what happens when we pour the dirty water and pebbles through this filter. Jesus is a filter for our sins. Jesus takes every sin away. Jesus cleans us and makes us right with God. If we ask Jesus to forgive our sins, He will.

(Remove the filter from the jar, keeping the pebbles inside. Hold up the filter full of pebbles.) When Jesus died on the cross, He took all of our sins into His own body, just like this filter did, so that we could be clean.

Prayer:

Thank you, Jesus, for dying for us. Please take our sins away. Amen.

Repentance

Scripture:
"If we confess our sins, he is faithful and just and will forgive us our sins and purify us from all unrighteousness" (1 John 1:9).

Object: pair of pants
You will need a pair of old pants with a grass stain.

(Show the children the pants with the grass stain. Ask if they have ever gotten grass stains on any of their clothing. Ask how it happened.)

When we fall in the grass, we are likely to end up with grass stains on our clothes. *(Hold up a household hints book or stain removal chart.)*
Some stains don't come out in the wash. Stains usually have to be cleaned in special ways. Some stains need to be washed in hot water and others need to be washed in cold water. Some stains need to be loosened with chemicals before they are washed. Stains need to be washed in special ways or they won't come out. This book tells how to get grass stains out of clothes. It also tells how to get out chocolate and catsup and ink stains. This is a very helpful book. *(Hold up a Bible.)*
This book also tells how to get out different kinds of stains. This book is a Bible. When we fall down in grass, we need a stain book to tell us how to remove the grass stain from our clothes. That's when we need a household stain book. But sometimes we fall down as Christians. When we do wrong things, it is like falling down. And when we fall, we get stains on our souls. That's when we need the Bible. In the Bible God tells us how to get the stains from doing wrong things off of our souls. The Bible tells us how our souls can be washed clean again. Can anyone tell us what the Bible says we need to do to get rid of the stains on our souls?

The Bible tells us that when we are sorry for doing a wrong thing we need to tell God what we did and then ask God to forgive us for doing wrong. If we do that, God has promised to wash away the stains on our souls and make us clean. Our stains will be washed away in a special way. Remember, when we are sorry for what we have done, we need to tell God and ask Him to forgive us. God will wash away what we have done. God will forgive us and make us clean.

Prayer:
Dear God, thank you for forgiving us when we do wrong. We are sorry for the times we have been selfish and unkind. Please forgive us and wash us clean. Amen.

Jesus Is the Truth

Scripture:
"Dear friends, do not believe every spirit, but test the spirits to see whether they are from God, because many false prophets have gone out into the world. This is how you can recognize the Spirit of God: Every spirit that acknowledges that Jesus Christ has come in the flesh is from God, but every spirit that does not acknowledge Jesus is not from God" (1 John 4:1-3).

Object: paper tube
For each child roll a piece of 8 1/2 X 11 paper lengthwise into a one inch tube. Secure the tube with tape

(Have the paper tubes in full view of the children.)

Someone once said, "Seeing is believing." What does that mean? (*Accept responses.*)
Some people believe that what we see is always true. But sometimes our eyes can play tricks on us. We should

not always believe what we see because what we see may just be a trick. Let me prove to you that seeing is not always believing. You can use these tubes of paper to play a trick with your eyes. *(Give each child one of the paper tubes.)*

Keep both of your eyes open and look through the tube with your right eye. *(Be sure tube is near right eye or trick will not work.)* Now put your left hand, palm up, in front of your left eye and stare straight ahead, not at your hand. Hold your left hand open next to the tube. Make your little finger touch the tube. *(Demonstrate.)* What do you see? *(There will appear to be a hole in the left hand.)*

Yes, it looks like you have a hole in your hand. Do you really have a hole in your hand? No, your eyes are just playing a trick on you. What we see is not always true.

Jesus warned us about tricks. He said that people might try to trick us into believing things that are not true. Jesus said not to believe everything we see and hear. The Bible says, "My dear friends: do not believe all who claim to have the Spirit, but test them to find out if the spirit they have comes from God. For many false prophets have gone out everywhere. This is how you will be able to know whether it is God's Spirit: anyone who acknowledges that Jesus Christ came as a human being has the Spirit who comes from God. But anyone who denies this about Jesus does not have the Spirit from God." (1 John 4:1-3 Good News Bible)

So, if anyone tells you that Jesus is not real, don't believe it. They are trying to trick you. God sent Jesus into the world to save us from our sins. Jesus said, "I am the truth."

Remember, you don't have a hole in your hand, but Jesus does. Jesus has holes in His hands because He died on the cross to save us from our sins. Jesus is the truth.

Prayer:

Jesus, we believe that you died on the cross to save us from our sins. You are real, and you are the truth. Amen.

Showing Love

Scripture:
"Dear friends, let us love one another, for love comes from God. Everyone who loves has been born of God and knows God. Whoever does not love does not know God, because God is love" (1 John 4:7, 8).

Object: celery

Two or three days before meeting with the children, prepare the celery. Cut the bottom ends from two stalks of celery which have the leaves left on. Place the stalks into jars of water. Add a few drops of red food coloring to the water in one of the jars and a few drops of blue food coloring to the water in the other jar. Display the jars of colored water and celery where the children can see them.

(Ask the children to observe the display carefully and then describe what they see. Ask them to explain what they think has happened in each instance.)

The colored water was drawn up through the stems and into the leaves. People are like these stalks of celery. Some people place themselves in God. They love God and He is in them, moving through their lives just like this red water moved through the stalk and up into the leaves of the celery. We can see the red water in the celery. We can see God in people, too. We can see God in every act of kindness. We can see God in the way a caring Christian lives.

But some other people are like this stalk of celery in the blue water. Some people love things instead of God. When we love things more than we love God, it shows in our lives just like this blue water shows in the celery leaves. When we love things more than we love God, we become selfish. Selfishness shows.

When we love God, we show that love in the way we live. When we love only things, it shows in the selfish way we live. Our lives show what we love. Christians need to love God and show His love in kindness and caring as they live and work with others.

Prayer:
Lord God, let our lives show your love in us. Help us show your kindness and caring to everyone. Amen.

Reading the Bible

Scripture:
"Blessed is the one who reads the words of this prophecy, and blessed are those who hear it and take to heart what is written in it, because the time is near" (Revelation 1:3).

Object: candy bars
Before class obtain enough small individually wrapped candy bars for each child in class to have one at the end of your talk. Put them in a clear plastic bag.

(Hold up the clear bag in which you have placed the candy bars.)

I really like to eat candy bars. As a matter of fact, one of these candy bars would be mighty tasty right about now. Before I can taste it and enjoy it, what will I need to do? *(Unwrap it.)*
(Open a candy bar and hold it up.) This is the good part. But before I could get to the good part and enjoy it, I had to do a little work. I had to open the wrapper.
The Bible is like a candy bar. The good part is inside. We can't enjoy the Bible unless we open it and read it. The good part is not the cover. The good part is inside. We can't enjoy a candy bar if we leave it in the cupboard. And we can't enjoy the Bible if we leave it on a table or shelf.
God gave us the Bible so we could open it up and read it and learn how to live in His goodness and love. What

could you do if you have trouble reading the words in the Bible by yourself? *(Accept responses.)* If you can't read the Bible by yourself, you can ask a grown-up or a bigger brother or sister to help you.

(Give each child one of the small candy bars to remember that we all need to open our Bibles to get to the good part just like we need to open a candy bar to get to the good part.)

Prayer:
Dear God, thank you for giving us the Bible to tell us how to live in your love. Help us remember to open our Bibles and read them. Amen.

Prayers Please God

Scripture:
"And when he had taken the scroll, the four living creatures and the twenty-four elders fell down before the Lamb. Each one had a harp and they were holding golden bowls full of incense, which are the prayers of the saints" (Revelation 5:8).

Object: candle
You will need a pleasantly scented candle for this talk.

(Hold up the candle for the children to see.)

This is a special candle because it is scented. When the candle burns, it makes a sweet smell. Let's try it. *(Light the candle.)*
When the candle is lit, it makes a sweet smell all of the time it is burning. This one is very fragrant. Can you smell it? It smells very good. What a delightful fragrance!
Did you know that when you pray, your prayers smell very good to God? Yes, God enjoys the fragrance of prayers. The Bible tells us that our prayers smell sweet and

that God saves our prayers in golden bowls. God must find your prayers very sweet and very important because when you send out a prayer to God He treasures it, saves it and delights in the sweet, sweet smell. God treasures your prayers. They make Heaven smell sweet.

Prayer:
Dearest God, may our prayers please you and make a sweet, sweet smell in your Heaven. Amen.